PHILOSOPHER AT THE
SKIN EDGE OF BEING

PHILOSOPHER AT THE SKIN EDGE OF BEING

SUSAN ANDREWS GRACE

Clarise Foster, Editor

Signature
EDITIONS

Cover design by Doowah Design.
Photo of Susan Andrews Grace by Jeremy Addington.

This book was printed on Ancient Forest Friendly paper.
Printed and bound in Canada by Hignell Book Printing Inc.

Acknowledgements
Many thanks for wisdom to Nicole Brossard during her prairie girl period; for encouragement and supper to Jennifer Craig, Anne de Grace, Joyce Macdonald and Verna Relkoff; for friendship and her eagle eye to Sylvia Legris; for that critical birthday phone call to Rusty Dixson; for her artful conversation to Elaine Muth; for thinking breakfasts to Vangie Bergum and for her quick and cosmic wit to Bobbie Ogletree.

Much appreciation goes to Clarise Foster for the vast background knowledge that she brought to the editing process.

Thanks to the Canada Council for the Arts for a mid-career grant near the beginning of this project and to the Saskatchewan Artists and Writers Colonies for space and time to work in 2008.

Thank you also to editors of the following publications in which earlier versions of poems appeared: *The Antigonish Review, Antioch Review, Canadian Literature, Grain Magazine, New Orphic Review, Prairie Fire, Smartish Pace.*

We acknowledge the support of The Canada Council for the Arts and the Manitoba Arts Council for our publishing program.

Library and Archives Canada Cataloguing in Publication

Grace, Susan Andrews
    Philosopher at the skin edge of being / Susan Andrews Grace.

Poems.
ISBN 978-1-927426-04-3

    I. Title.

PS8563.R31P55 2013   C811'.54   C2013-901018-1

Signature Editions
P.O. Box 206, RPO Corydon, Winnipeg, Manitoba, R3M 3S7
www.signature-editions.com

for Gord Andrews

Introduction

Meet Jia-li, a sort of everywoman at the centre of *Philosopher at the Skin Edge of Being*. She's an ideal woman in a Platonic sense. Jia-li is the philosopher feminine, a designation I've made up just as I've imagined Jia-li into being. The philosopher feminine is a problematic, as the French philosophers would have it, a matrix that shares some edges with the poet. Edges that overlap strengthen cloth and may also strengthen idea. Jia-li lives in a North American, mountainous, interior rainforest. She represents the metaphysician in everyone: she wonders about being, existence, reality and beauty. In fact, her name means beauty in Mandarin. Jia-li balances a world shaped, in part, by two sages, Plotinus and Laozi, whom you will also meet in this book.

Plotinus, founder of Neo-Platonism, was a third-century philosopher whose thinking was clarification, in his mind, of Plato's philosophy. Plotinus was Egyptian-born, educated in Alexandria, and taught in Rome until his death, after which his life's work, *The Enneads*, was collected and published by his student, Porphyry. The appearance of *The Enneads*, six groups of nine tractates, marks an important juncture because the Church adopted Neo-Platonism via Augustine, shaping the Western world. *The Enneads* were also taken up by the Islamic world but attributed to Aristotle. Irish journalist Stephen MacKenna used up his life gloriously, translating *The Enneads* from Greek in the early twentieth century, the first time *The Enneads* was translated into English in its entirety.

Laozi (aka Lao Tzu, Lao Tse, etc), whose name, however spelled, means "old master," lived in the sixth century BCE. He was founder of Daoism and author of the *Daodejing* or *Tao Te Jing*. *Dao* means "way," *de* "virtue," and *jing* "classic." The story goes that Laozi, an archivist, was leaving the city of Chu in disgust at its corruption when a sentry stopped him at the northwest gate and demanded Laozi's wisdom. The result of that conversation was the *Daodejing*, which, next to the Bible, is the most translated book in the world and could be said to be Daoism's holy book. Its 81 short poems that give timeless advice to rulers, sages and ordinary people on first glance seem as easy to read as *The Enneads* is not, but the poems are complex and sometimes puzzling.

Plato and Laozi were roughly contemporaries in a world where West was West and East was East. At the same time that Plotinus was becoming the father of Neo-Platonism there was a Neo-Daoism happening in China. Plotinus greatly desired to go east, most likely India and/or Persia, and travelled part-way with the Roman army but was sent back. Laozi got as far as the northwest gate of his city, as far as we know, although according to lore, he wanted to go west. They never met, but their thinking might meet or indeed overlap.

Laozi is the Chinese echo in Jia-li's world as she practices Daoism's central tenet, *wu wei* which means non-action, doing the right and natural thing, without controlling. *Wu wei* is represented by water which, though soft, can teach stone and move mountains. Jia-li sees the evidence of *wu wei* in her world daily, just as she recognizes beauty from within, as Plotinus advises. She contemplates beauty and makes of her self a statue, cutting away and smoothing the lines of her inner being so that it too reflects beauty and she can see it in the realities of her existence.

The Enneads and the *Daodejing* were written for free men of an elite class; women and girls were never expected to read them. And Jia-li probably hasn't. But she could if she wanted to, and I bet she will when you shut this book.

Imagining how the philosopher imagines is one way to read and learn a philosophy. Most likely Plotinus imagined Plato thinking. This imagining suits the practice of poetry, as well. A philosopher at the skin edge of being is the poet whose imagining takes a turn into sound, which travels around corners. Jia-li knows light needs a mirror to take that turn. The poet knows she can mirror philosophy, finding its beauty as thought overcomes difficulty.

I

The Good is gentle, mild, and very delicate, and always at the
disposition of whomever desires it.
— Plotinus
The Enneads, V.12.33-35

The softest things in the world ride roughshod over the hardest things.
Only the least substantial things can penetrate the seamless.
This is how we know that doing things noncoercively is beneficial.
— Laozi
Daodejing, Chapter 43

I

1

Ice falls off a mountain

water molecules sleek with movement.

Jia-li, however numbed by existential blows of aggression,
sees truth in some lies, reaches into the muddle,
plucks ethereal pomegranates
split, red and succulent:

what is possible is not always obvious.

I | 2

Jia-li mediates skin, her house,
earth's equilibrium under a coverlet of snow,
moon's borrowed light.

She breathes inside the frost of day's knitting
       beauty survives danger,
       kingliness rules virtue

      in human intellect.

Jia-Li's mountains
slippery with spring
intersect lake's horizon.

I | **3**

Before death this:
>   terraced farmland and oiled oxen,
>   blue silk jacket over bare skin,
>   a bloody tent.

Watery cells respond to a bright full moon
dropped through the bedroom window—
>   mind says *Sleep*— *Yes, Yes!*

Jia-li returns to morning, organs pinked,
bones stardust, her knit body
ready for duty, unlike those who died in their sleep last night—
>   the ones who knew which heaven.

I | 4

Behind a face, under the hair—
speed of light in tulips, their burst red opening—

      bleed black powder
      upon a white table.

The tulip's force to flower
crosses invisibly—

      pulls Jia-li by the hair.

I | 5

Jia-li contemplates green river pools, blue alfalfa
ghosts live deep under the bridge where it squeezes the bank.

Soul wears
a jade bracelet, just as Jia-li does, and
rides a white swan through water and air
astride its feathered back.

Earth is heaven's hotel room,
occupied by souls as they contemplate the world,
consider how best to dress its wounds,
bless the snow, encourage grasses.

I | **6**

Presence of the mother came before all other fierceness
      contains wine's ruby breath,
      nasturtium's wet seeds,
      soaked indigo heavens,
      warmth of new wool.

Mother opens the floodgates —
      arteries release scarlet
      return of roiling oxygen to air's
      leak of chlorophyll, as grass knits
      earth's immaculate underground.

Grass comes before

and will reclaim.

I | 7

A baby swims out of darkest sea
a cloud-kissed tiger tamer,
safe from eagles.

I | 8

Whether we peel a birch or mulberry tree for its paper
or a palm tree for its barkcloth, we humans mark it.

Nature treats us as palmcloth, birchbark:
we rot, given time.

    The skull carries a mirror made of skin:

reflects stars along a North American stream-fed lake
or warm springs of Egyptian oases.

Mind tries to make soul jealous.

I | **9**

Each time raw beauty startles, soul reminds stars,
     of violets nestled in green grass,
     morning scent of cottonwood
     and pine, oxygen roiling—
pleasures bridge matter's river.

A philosopher looks to the day with tenderness —
     she knows the world
     begrudges nothing.

I | **10**

Plotinus advises we cultivate astonishment
at the extraordinary and the ordinary.

An orchid in its black pot on an English oak chest, in a Plotinian world,
as important as the dandelion's yellow crown of brilliant teeth.

Both have capacity to save a soul.

I | *

In skin time, Jia-li picks daffodils, in mountain's breath, bare feet wet with dew. A soul, half-asleep with Diet Coke in hand, may leave the kitchen for the backyard in full moonlight to look at daffodils for reasons of divinity. A puddle on the patio reflects Jia-li and the moon behind her. Scared awake, she wonders: who leads in this confederacy of incarnation?

A soul could nearly drown in the matter of embodiment just as Jia-li could drown in the matter of ensoulment. The latter is preferable, but no escape. The best recourse for Jia-li— to give puddles and daffodils to the sun, go back to bed until morning.

II
—

Every soul is, and becomes, that which she contemplates.
—Plotinus
The Enneads, IV.3.8

The nameless is the fetal beginnings of everything that is happening,
while that which is named is their mother.
—Laozi
Daodejing, Chapter 1

II | 1

Seize the great image and the world will flock to you.
$$\text{Chapter 35, } Daodejing$$

We, like oxen, will be eaten by worms or fire—

    draught animals who take refuge
    lands of language and form

marry our cravings and try, in spite of its yoke
to seize the *great image* in confusion—
    multitudes of idea.

We seek *gentle mild and very delicate* goodness;
require as oxen do, grasses and groundwater,
carry the fire that will eat us,
        work to spend our flesh.

This, the sages agree,
preferable to cravings
that consume us.

II | **2**

If you are lucky, Plotinus said, Athena
or some other goddess will pull you by the hair
                turn you
to face the sumptuous world.

                       And you will see inside everything, even
your face sewn in fine stitches of blood,
bone and cartilage
                orderly support.

That which connects all faces is the nature of wisdom:
                a vessel determines its own capacity.

We cannot add or subtract
skin's containment
nor impose upon it
                without sorrow.

II | 3

What rises in love does so without fear:
      beauty ascends to marry good,
        iridescence that shimmers in this world.

Jia-li is as certain of this as she is of the buzzing bee
dashing its existence against walls and screens
then stings her.

II | 4

Names of the gods in Jia-Li's geographies
are thick with meaning, stumbling in a junky desert.
Beer bottles litter in their millions, brown glass
sparkles on the horizon.
Joshua trees fall over like drunks outside the Mojave bar, bayonet cacti
slashed by heat and nesting birds.

Soul rescues vagrancy.

Jia-Li dreams she gives the ocean
her pearl earrings and bolts of silk,
yellow and blue, for sun and sky—

throws baubles and ashes to the waves as she rides

her swan, singing white feathers and air,
her whole self riding the bird,
standing the ocean.

II | 5

Grasping oneness is not unlike
understanding a pair of pants—
two legs identically opposed but united by a crotch seam.
No greater glory (under normal circumstances) ascribed to the right
or left leg, the front seam, back seam, side pocket or back pocket.

Each part of the whole and the whole necessary
to keep a human clothed. Pants serve the wearer, who is Jia-Li,
and who sometimes wears a skirt. Plato would say
pants are a mere reflection. Jia-Li would say *They better not be!*

She demands, in the twenty-first century, the best idea of pants
in the ones she wears. Plotinus would say pants reflect oneness
in that they are cotton which grew in the Nile's delta
and under its sun, transformed from fluff

into string, then woven and sewn and of course, these pants—
measures of cloth—participate in the whole.
We must be grateful for and contemplate every bitty bit of these pants,
and add to that, gratitude for coverage.

In this way we will grasp oneness, its embrace of the lower body,
its contribution to well-being, and its protection from
the scratch of long grasses.

    Laozi says *Sages grasp oneness to be shepherd to the world.*

We imagine him, fed up with the antics of his people,
Laozi, leaving this idea behind
wearing a seamless cotton garment
as he deserts his city, forever.

II | 6

The lesson each night—

  how fragile life &
  tenuous our hold

as cells whisper in morning
   it's lonely out there
that union of particularities.

Look now to forest canopies—
   angels and ghosts
   do nothing for you.

II | 7

Traces of intelligence in wood disappear
when the tree's fullness is invaded.

Matter wears form, Plotinus would say. Laozi warns
trouble for individual and nation:
                    fullness depleted will cause confusion.

Inaction leads to fullness
and contemplation:

on this Plotinus and Laozi would agree
and a tree still stands.

II | 8

The baby girl forgets where she came from.
A young woman has long forgotten, the middle-aged woman
wonders where all these creatures, human and otherwise,
come from.

An old woman contemplates return but
the wise woman has one ear cocked for clues,

eyes on the road ahead: tansy August ditches
and amber evening as
                        she walks in unity of consciousness
knows the walk will not last—
winds of mourning soon enough,

purity her duty in consciousness.

This will not last a day
as it takes her life.

II | 9

Jia-li's face reflects eternity:
only face she'll ever have.

❙

A riverbed-god knows things, takes knowledge
to the new moon's scant light.

❙

A blade of grass or the moon are contemplated
not designed into being, said Plotinus.

❙

Plotinus thought the gods should come to him,
not up to him to go to the gods.

❙

Jia-li abandons the gods to love's body,
this short tenure, contemplation.

II | 10

The one or the good is beyond grasp—

impossible to fill or to empty.

The whole is breath and wears its skin.

Plotinus's thought aligned with Laozi's

> *what's perfectly full seems empty*
> *but you can't use it up.*

II | 11

At death, soul shakes off embodiment,
plays music without her instrument.

There is no opposite to music as hate is opposite to love,
beauty to ugliness. Music takes opposites in tones,
makes correspondences and harmony,
lets the note sing a child's clear voice.

This is the word of Plotinus, concurring in music with Laozi—
       sages who develop what's given, but do not initiate,
       give an account of what's true or beautiful
       with an open hand.

II | 12

Joy rises as steam from a cup of tea reminds
the philosopher's heart of beauty's reach,

evil rendered harmless
in the roil of being.

II | **13**

A person free and fed well
thinks with wings.

        Cells march,
contemplation delights—
                the peach most its self when its skin,
tight around peachness, hangs from the branch.

The philosopher who sees this
through a green leaf screen
is most her self.

II | 14

Mysticism arises out of misery. This remains a social fact.

The most destitute centuries produce seismic change,
to benefit the miserable and everyone else.

A wise teacher says little but observes what is not discussed,
reaches indeterminate humanity to rest her case:

> rose in summer dawn so perfectly white
> a vein of pink threatens to shatter the cosmos,
> its velvet canyon.

II | 15

The one and the way are alike— inexhaustible.

Plotinus's stream that never runs dry, boiling

life, flows with blood in a subtle universe—

bodies of a baby, mother, father, dog, cat, mouse,

demand respect: the mouse

snack-food in the wild,

humans specks in the universe.

II | 16

The road up a mountain of sepulchres
slices death with switchbacks.

Intellect communicates with intellect, while first mind
carries our blue sphere sewn into a fold of its tunic,

a hole in galactic conversation
mended by rain.

II | 17

Heaven treats us like dogs, which explains human morality

regarding dogs, as if dogs cared.

        The philosopher looks

for a river, finds friendly dogs as she carries beneath

her dawn-reddened cloak a poet's heart.

She wants to make something of river reeds,

a kingfisher's flight, sun's stripes on morning.

Dogs run in a pack to greet her, as if she was someone

they knew. Dogs have no religion.

II | **18**

For death there is no consolation:

ravelled attention to the river,

walks in early morning.

II | 19

Plotinus and the Chinese sages agree:
woman is "the root of the world"

      fecundity of human existence;
      she is negative; the destructive force of birth;
      pain bringing forth fruits of imperfect love.

Her other lips are always to blame:
they kiss the mud, need domination.

The Mud Queen, a slithering and shiny idea,
kept Plotinus awake all night,
pulled him through shoals of the Nile like a siren of intellect
so that in morning his box of books and the other box of clothing
bound with rope ready to go to Rome,
confronted him.

              The boat had already left—
but he heard what the muddy lips sang and was joyous.
He would follow their tremolos the rest of his life or
until he found what he was looking for.

A girl philosopher already knows.

II | 20

Consider the five-year-old girl who walks with her father
down a dusty road in hot sun, trusting
she will return to her mother that night
to sleep with her sister in a warm nest on the dirt floor,
eat *jook* porridge in the morning.

❚

Consider Plotinus, advisor to the emperor
who marches from Syria to the river Euphrates
contemplating imageless truth, unaware of thirst or hunger.

❚

Consider Plotinus's slave, who finds mules to carry boxes of clothing
and books, pitches the tent, cooks at night and does it
in a storm of silence, his ear, like a seashell, knows
only the distant ocean roar.

❚

The girl will not return with her father, her grief
to be soothed by strangers.

Plotinus will never arrive at his destination.

The deaf slave does not own his future and so cannot lose it.

II | 21

Festering wounds of battle, bandaged tides of pus
drown compassion for wounded citizens
who bleed with identical agony.
Breath, movement, and thought embroider pain,
starved for oxygen as it rips and shoots the face with tracery
of what's unbearable.
                    A philosopher lies in the crook of healing
as if it were a tree.

II | **22**

Cleopatra loved silk. When Plotinus travelled back from Persia,
silk was new and scandalous in Rome. Formless shimmer,
pure light of a blue-edged cloud—
silk veils a lover with divinity, diaphanous
cloth of the godhead and flowers,
conferred royalty to the senses.

Silk brought danger to the empire.

II | **23**

Lit villas along the river Ostia, Plotinus said
are like dresses on fire, lace in the air,

feminine deities move their arms into spacious sleeves,
fill and give shape to life— naked and clothed.

▌

As the soul, so the body.

▌

Skin wears contemplation,
mind's shelter.

II | 24

Perhaps the best city for philosophy
will rid its self of poets. Plato thought so.

Plotinus knew, however, that Plato
would have kept the poetry of banished poets
in his perfect city. He had no use for theft.

Plotinus imagined porches for poetry and philosophy to meet
past twilight, lying side by side on mats, conversing as
dark clambers and stars punch
blue-black firmament with fire.

       At dawn,
poetry and philosophy still on the porch, will
share a breakfast of dew-red mulberries,
bless their city of men, women, and slaves—
and the girl philosopher in the garden that morning.

II | **25**

Heaven's river causes no anxiety, has no favourites,
flows in generosity of a teacher like Plotinus,

rapturous presence to his students. Summer,
like heaven's river, ripens fruit under their skins—

minds become compassion. The philosopher does not stand
on the river bank, she swims into summer's teaching.

II | **26**

Even though we may peer into contemplation's

back room where silver machinery pumps thought and idea

inaudible, intangible formlessness,

we know there is a further back room— a kitchen

cooking wedding breakfasts.

And we know souls

remember formless delight.

II 27

The married daughter leaves her father an empty house:
    a bride's communion with her mother
    remembers inch by milky inch in white writing
    her hair ebony tumbles down her back,
    thought inscribed to loss.

II | 28

A stone glistens smooth as water that polishes,
just as compassion erodes sorrow.

Sun and moon rule sky.

Plotinus wrote that one must have discipline and not complain—
but he comforted those who suffered.

Pain polishes this contrariness. The girl philosopher
carries pebbles in her pockets, heart clarified.

II | **29**

The soul stays with a body to keep it whole, said Plotinus.

Wildflowers interrupted by grasses bow in the wind:
the only undivided thing is change:

Our own particle of intellect dispersed in the cosmos,
as salt mingles with water —
both change and un-change.

We know pavement under our feet, and
heaven in skin's cells, ripened heads of grass,
daisy spheres, and bluebells
bent as if to ring.

II | 30

Water sifts sand and rock. Earth recognizes its
molecules, watery intelligence
ascends in mist.

  This, Laozi and Plotinus agree,
has to do with soul's governance of body and earth.

  We love water, need and follow its dance,
trace its valleys to sea.

II |
    *

A soul who has lost her way also loses that which sent her. Jia-li comes to, fridge door open, shivers in its draught. Jia-li will not satisfy soulfulness or her body's need for calcium to build bones, teeth, nails, and strength: she chooses a can of Diet Coke. What soul buys Diet Coke in the first place, you ask? A soul that wants a glamorous body; the body that's lost its gleam and trades it for safety. And for this reason alone, a mystical marriage of *wu wei* and Plato's daughter of heaven makes sense, Jia-li thinks. She cheats the soul of breath, lets earth find her.

III

We encounter the extraordinary with astonishment, though we
should be astonished at these ordinary things too.
—Plotinus
The Enneads IV.4.37

It is for this reason that sages know
without going anywhere out of the ordinary,
understand clearly without saying anything out of the ordinary
and get things done without doing anything out of the ordinary.
—Laozi
Daodejing, Chapter 4

III | 1

Soul must be free to conquer existence,
gather up her full taffeta skirt and
whisper carmine history.

Soul makes life long whether the body lives or not.
Jia-li celebrates yellow mats of October leaves,
rains which pelt and bounce on roadways.

Sages may be seamstresses, gather children and men around them,
ruffling change, wearing bracelets.

III │ 2

Laozi leaves town, sure that everything carries *yin*
on its shoulder and *yang* in its arms, and this
secret harmony: dialectic of the one and the many.

Plotinus, if he were on the road with Laozi, might point to the grassy
roadside, the cow in the field and to the venerable Laozi as well
to say *You are right and you are wrong.* There is no one and many
there is only one-many and so you, Laozi,
are much bigger than you think:
you are more, just as the cow and the grass are more.
There is only one soul,
all souls present in us.

Laozi would beg his pardon and say *But that is what I said already*
flicking a fly from his shoulder with his long baby fingernail.
And they'd sit down in the dusty road to talk some more
or until forced off the byway, whichever came first. Plotinus
happy, at long last, to have met the east.

III |
3

A philosopher's drunkenness,
heavy with nectar—
>   like a bee's contentment in the garden,
>   crumpled energy a jumble of generosity,
>   and pollen insurance

redeems wastrel ways.

III | 4

The philosopher knows our bodies are crucibles of dust,
soul their spark of belonging.

Between god and no-god is safety of the universe.

Nothing that belongs to the all can be discarded by it,
says Plotinus.
The universe is trustworthy.

An insect eating her way through the magnolia leaves
and a girl belong to this magnificence: the garden shone upon
by a red sun through smoky skies, by a low-hung
white moon, and by striped Leonid showers.

Despair sits on the edge of the bed
feet dangling, midnight, and cold
mountain air cools the house
for another hot day tomorrow.

III | 5

Helpless to bring order to any state as a baby is to cook a fish,

Neo-Platonism and Daoism remain equally

      inefficient, inelegant, and lonesome.

Forces of greed and fear pay no attention

hush of cloud, pink bleed,

blue sky.

The one,

wu wei, and snow—

      equally fallen.

III | 6

The birch tree will one day fall, its bark
studded with lesions, blackened branches reach
to a bleached sky.
After death the tree will be buried by forest's industry
and worker beings, insects and birds,
to renew what lived:
particular form.

III | 7

Regarding Plotinus's teaching on matter:

> To subtract form from matter, lie in the grass all day long. Subtract the sun. Stay there until the moon rises, then subtract it and the stars and collect them in the compost heap of intellect: they will not be wasted. Then looking into that emptiness, subtract also the earth upon which you are lying. And then subtract your body too, as it has no place to rest anyway. What good is it to you now? Matter has disappeared.

The philosopher asks *Has your soul collapsed or is it still under construction?* The jangle of hidden power survives existence, burning-glass upon intellect's peregrination.

III | 8

To surrender the body at death, existence

must push consciousness off the mountain,

watch it flounder in the talus, leave

skin's shroud in gravel.

Existence is the emptiness Plotinus
and a girl philosopher seek.

Plotinus, his throat scaled with lesions, his whisper hoarse,

returned the divine he had seen along the river Nile.

Mud Queen kissed him as the snake

slipped into a hole in the wall of his chamber,

Plotinus's body, property of the universe,

remained.

III | 9

The day Plotinus died, Rome's oldest woman
poured wisdom into salt— her bath floaty
with seawater, kelp, and lavender.

      She rose, ready for gold rings
and purple silk:

      thunder and lightning.

Stars in her tapestry haunted the other side.

Jia-li sees the one true screen,
centuries between

a girl in the garden.

III | **10**

A snail shell stripped to beauty
on the school house stairs
curves into the mind of Jia-li.
The snail shrugged his house,
flesh no longer luminous,
the hard excess of his life
remains absolutely without
coral space as testament
to emptiness.
Mass stays
shell of snail idea.

III | 11

The many is contained in the one. Plotinus could tell which slave had stolen the necklace of a woman in his household. He saw crime in the man's eyes.

We all participate. Even though a sea contains water of its tributaries, water always remains its self.

Laozi would say that naming such a process is dangerous. When we know without naming and we act from the heart, heaven rains sweetness. The slave would not need to steal a necklace in the first place and Plotinus would not have had the slave flogged until he produced it.

If Jia-Li were in heaven with Plotinus and Laozi, drinking tea, she would see how much sadness could be prevented had they met here, in this, her heaven.

III | 12

Regarding Plotinus's pacificism—

open the gate of your being to what was before
    —being and not being—
      find that which is
      and was always.

That way, says Plotinus
      (and Laozi nods in agreement),
you will never need again.

Death will bring a basket of nosegays
        smelling salts for being,
      to remind you
            Wake up!

For now
    skin's spacetime.

III | 13

A bit of fancy, this heaven, where Laozi and Plotinus
meet over tea to discuss the good.
                              To keep peace
Laozi does not mention pacificism.

                    They agree on many things,
including tea's medicinal properties,
relative condition of the sky's blueness
and importance of pain as a teacher.

There is no aggression and no military—
just order, happiness and desire.
Sages know history, as do Laozi and Plotinus.

Their talk could rescue us,
over tea.

III | 14

To access goodness, thought is the best instrument.

A bread-baking oven vastly superior
to the semi-automatic rifle,
in securing happiness.

A society which goes to war, said Laozi
and celebrates weapons becomes sorry.
To glorify killing
engage careless thought:

bold intellection best alternative to killing.

III

*

Soul arrives at the bus stop before the body has finished brushing his teeth, before he, puffing and wheezing, catches up just as the Greyhound slows in a cloud of dust to take body and soul from this backwoods into the eternal present. Sun kisses ruby horizon as the bus driver pulls away, cracking his gum, and the door hisses closed. The philosopher willingly finds a seat, lurching as she does, to the right then the left, as gears shift on understanding. Soul knows light, which fills it by eliminating everything that is not light. In ancient China this process of ditching all darkness and grays would be the light a Plotinian soul sought in the first place.

III
**

Plotinus claimed Gnostics were high-handed and working on the wrong plane: they put soul before intellect. Gnostics believed they lived *there* and belonged *there* but had no logical explanation as to why they were *here*. If Plotinus and the Chinese sages were on Rex Murphy's "Cross Country Check-Up" they might agree that contemplation brings a kind of ecstasy but there's still responsibility to use one's head, to think. Plotinus would exhort caller Canadians, in his quiet and modest way, tubercular flesh rotting as he spoke to not be fooled by a United Nations' proclamation of Canada as the best of countries. But to look instead at what they consider beneath them, to lower the ladder of reality to a horizontal position, parallel to grassy plains, green rugs under which broken civilizations have been swept for centuries— and think about what that means, and how it can be true that we are a young nation. Chinese sages, always pragmatic, reeling from tubercular stench would agree but plead first for comfort, ask Rex to do something about the smelly Roman, transplanted from Egypt. Opening a window is impossible in a CBC studio— they'd go to tape.

IV

Being is desirable because it is identical with Beauty, and Beauty is
loved because it is Being.
—Plotinus
The Enneads, V.8.9

Way-making is so profuse as to be nameless.
It is only way-making that is as efficacious in the beginnings of things
as it is in their completion.
—Laozi
Daodejing, Chapter 41

IV | 1

You wouldn't be the first person to use a pillow for a shield,
Jia-li tells herself as she awakens
feeling foolish.

She holds the pillow in front of her, fights
her Don Quixote on his spindly wind horse—
not even a Rosinate, Jia-Li knows

Don Quixote only wants to love her,
or so he says. Jia-li asks questions, skeptical
but tempted. He's beginning to look more and more
like Santa Claus in summer—sweaty and red,
no white beard but many gifts for her.
She keeps protecting herself.

IV | 2

Eight Treasures tea in the thick squat cup set before Jia-li—
    Wolfberries, Chinese Dates, Chrysanthemum blossom,
    honeysuckle, and lychee swim brightly in yellow.

This cup is nothing in Plotinian eternity
and Jia-li's body is dust.

Red berries sluice through the spout,
each pour, each sip
closer to earth.

IV | 3

Snowberries rival snow,
winter leaves mad melt

celebrate weakening light
white rounds plump up black angles,
abandoned by leaves.

A snowberry returns determinate to indeterminate,
        from what is known to what isn't
        just as snow's miracle comes again
whether Jia-Li trusts or not.

IV | 4

First snow laces trees, pads fence posts, blankets roads and hills
and every vista. Though Plotinus knew beauty's permanence
and though he never saw snow, he would have known insensibly
its possibility and potential even though
his breath was never stolen for that second of its image piercing his eye,
his lungs never stabbed with cold.

IV | 5

Whining and complaining are necessary but not important—

sometimes acts performed without benefit.

Plotinus's idea, a city of Plato's philosophy, Platonopolis

abandoned. Plotinus's soul ascended,

his body joined life itself,

surrendered good and evil.

The Chinese sage would say Plotinus acted well on behalf of himself—

he gratefully returned divinity, not squandered.

IV | 6

Before ancestral gods there was a way. At the same time
there was the one.

Since the one is all, the one must have known the way, perhaps
even used it.

Snowberries plump up, hard and firm with frost and poison,

contain all colour in waxy white:

> warm red and scarlet, indigo, violet, and purple
> words flutter like feathers from a Roman pillowcase,
> turned inside-out.

The way is for creatures and for earth, whether black and white
with frost

or baked red with iron. The one is what a philosopher contemplates

when snowberries arrest her on a cold morning, as the wolverine

forwardly gallops to water. Philosopher at the skin edge of being,

part of one and many, knows a way.

IV | 7

Gods worship night's harem.
A girl philosopher will have forgotten such dreams
by Egyptian daybreak.

Desert wind makes palm trees wave
against failing lapis to teach
winter's clarity.

IV | 8

What if Plotinus had seen snow, not just a mirage
of desert sand and heat
but real cold with deep blue in its white?

And what if his sister had demanded to read, pinned her brother's
body on the veranda floor, wrestled him for the codices?

What if she'd brought Plotinus back to the house to accelerate
his learning: witness life leave his mother's body, time's
comfort a blanket of roadside snow.

How Plotinus might have taught had his sister demanded—
how he might have understood, had he seen snow.

IV | **9**

The eye focuses on creek's ions as the observer invades its secret
known already to deer and mice, crow and sparrow,
and an owl further in the forest.

The inner eye registers creek and rock,
soft ground lush with melted snow, but ignores
change wrought by looking: tender grass trampled,

mossy cushions flattened, lichens that shelter leftover spaces
remain steadfast, as they always do, brighter for having been seen.

Mind pricks itself open, alerted to water trickling,

records, preserves: eye full of spring—
birds sing urgently, swoop and rush, busy with scraps and sticks.

The inner eye knows what to keep, what to let go.

IV | 10

Laozi says the way will safeguard those who are inept.

Plotinus asks *How shall we find the way?* (I.6.8)

Jia-li enters beauty, disciplined to clear away what is not smooth,
straighten what is crooked and
comprehend the dark un-seeable. Wonder's texture,
ordinary way of all cells,
keeps her.

IV | 11

Jia-li knows how large a clove of garlic and sliver of ginger,
how small the puffed-up pound of kale makes surface larger,
hunger smaller, satisfaction deep, and healing deeper.

Soul informs cuisine, heart under the apron removes difficulty,
recognizes goodness.

IV | 12

A person suited to rule the world is the best boarder
in the most excellent boarding house. She passes the butter
before being asked, contributes to conversation,
elicits talk from the shyest, and when the house catches fire
organizes safe rescue and escape of every occupant,
including the gentleman whose cigarette started the fire
and whose loud snoring off the rum
indicates he is still asleep.
The best boarder sleeps lightly, her vigilance awakened
gases filling the top third of air
                          leaps quickly with compassion.

IV | 13

The greater battle occurs between
good in life and desire for good in all of life.

Good has left the colosseum, except in remnants:
moral beginnings, sunny afternoon of birth, milky pact

between mother and newborn, as olive groves
promise riches. A tally completed and discarded in the colosseum:

an elephant's memory of her Egyptian mother's warmth
dies with her skin, their account closed.

IV | **14**

A baby remembers skin without breath
as she burps ambrosia, surveys idea from her perch on a shoulder.

      The baby's love of wisdom years away
      or not

ability to smile around the corner:
        she looks into the eyes of a sleep-
        walking parent
        begins descent into form.

      She expects leadership.

IV | 15

The philosopher as a small girl presses her forehead to eternity, sees
what the daemon urges: cosmos a Chinese goblet, renewing emptiness:
never-filled, brimming experience.

A girl confirms wisdom as she draws circles
in Egyptian sand with her bare foot, sun's warmth on tawny legs,
vessel of her brainpan fills with sky, sun's eye a pinhole to light
found by reason.

IV | 16

A philosopher learns from silence
and its consequences, her ears open to
celestial transcription.

IV | 17

The philosopher walks slender night
filled with dog shapes as she secrets poems,

scraps of papyrus, under her cloak. A philosopher
loves the poem, knows its danger resides in seduction.

Poems fly to the exact space where heaven
becomes earth and earth heaven.

Reason has not brought the philosopher along the river:
her mind is on wings and flies ahead.

A body contemplates when it sleeps. Knowledge is the unkept promise,
and disappointment day's bedrock.

IV | **18**

In old-growth swirls of cedar and lacy hemlock feathers,
trees are honoured as small children value parents—
assuming they exist for their use alone.

                        We inhabit beauty effortlessly,
name Lodgepole Pine for our uses
            structures with windows, doors and mouldings.

A tree's hundred years cut down in alignment with hierarchies
fail the pine which grows in adversity, after fire burns
thousand-year old cedar, eight-hundred-year-old hemlock.

Plotinus would agree with Laozi that beauty teaches
as long as we take beauty within, push out what stops virtue,
burn mind's detritus, and become vision.

Then we are desire
                    first to know, then to be:
                    droopy hemlock, wounded cedar.

Notes

Epigraph: Gwendolyn MacEwen: "Letters to Josef in Jerusalem, ii" *Afterworlds* Toronto: McClelland and Stewart, 1987

Epigraph: Lyotard, Jean Francois, *La Mur du Pacifique* in *The Lyotard Reader*, Edited by Andrew Benjamin and translated by Peter Brocket, Nick Royle, and Kathleen Woodward, Oxford: Blackwell, 1989

Epigraph: Susan Howe: *The Midnight*, p.115

"Sages grasp oneness to be shepherd to the world." Chapter 22, (p.110) *Daodejing "Making This Life Significant:" A Philosophical Translation*. Roger T. Ames and David L. Hall. (New York: Ballantine Books, 2003)

"gentle mild and very delicate" Plotinus, *The Enneads*, V.5.12, 33-35

All quotes from the *Daodejing* are from *Daodejing "Making This Life Significant:" A Philosophical Translation*. Roger T. Ames and David L. Hall. (New York: Ballantine Books, 2003)

ECO-AUDIT
Printing this book using Rolland Opaque 50
instead of virgin fibres paper saved the following resources:

Trees	Solid Waste	Water	Air Emissions
1	60 kg	1,969 L	183 kg